television

automobile

Some words are long words.

dinosaur

restaurant

Some words are short words.

Some words are fancy words.

carrousel

poodle

delicatessen

Some words are dancy words.

hula hoop

hokey pokey

ballet

Some words are prancy words.

tango

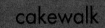

cakewalk

strut

cheerleader

Some words are antsy words.

jelly

Some words are fancy, dancy, prancy, antsy words.

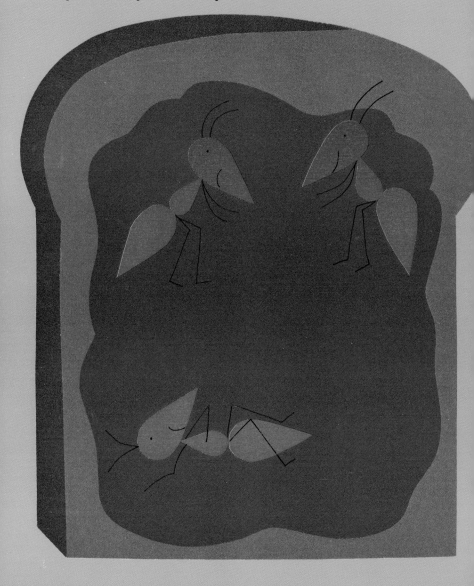